juices and smoothies

live life · be healthy · love life

juices and smoothies

live life · be healthy · love life

igloo

Published in 2007 by Igloo Books Ltd
Cottage Farm, Sywell, NN6 0BJ
www.igloo-books.com

The publisher, author, and editor have made every
reasonable effort to ensure that the recipes in this book
are safe when made as instructed but assume no
responsibility for any damage caused or sustained while
making recipes in this book.

ISBN: 978 1 84561 328 0
10 9 8 7 6 5 4
Printed in China

Project management: Toucan Books

Author: Jacqueline Bellefontaine
Design and layout: Bradbury and Williams
Editor: Theresa Bebbington
Photography: Andrew Sydenham © Toucan Books
Proofreader: Marion Dent

Contents

1
Life-Enhancing Drinks

"Juices" and "smoothies" are the new buzz words in the kitchen and for good reason too. For some time we have been told how important it is to eat a minimum of five fruit and vegetables every day. This is because they are packed full of the vitamins and minerals as well as the fibre that are required as part of a healthy diet. Juices and smoothies are a fun and tasty way of helping us to achieve this goal.

Homemade freshness

By making juices and smoothies yourself you will be ensuring that you get the maximum nutritional benefits from the fruit and vegetables. Shop-brought juices – even freshly squeezed juices – will have been in the bottle for several days, and in that time, the vitamin content will decrease. By making your own juices, you will know exactly what is in your drink, making it easier to avoid any additives. You may also prefer to use organic produce, thus ensuring that you are not inadvertently drinking any possible pesticide residues.

Curative powers

Juices have been used by herbalists and naturopaths for centuries to alleviate ailments and help prevent illness, and today many dieticians and nutritionists recommend including them in our diet. Juices and smoothies are a good way of consuming valuable antioxidants found in fruit and vegetables. Antioxidants help to protect our bodies against diseases and are important for the immune system.

Juices are also believed to be beneficial in many areas of health, from reducing stress and improving digestive health to helping build muscle and bone strength. The greater variety of fruit and vegetables in the diet, the more chance you have of consuming all the health-giving elements you'll need. If you tend to be a "meat and two veg person", making juices and smoothies is an easy way of extending the repertoire of fruit and vegetables you consume.

Whether you make juices and smoothies for health reasons or for fun, one thing is for certain – they are delicious and a great way of including fruit and vegetables in your diet.

Nutrition in a Nutshell

Smoothies vs. juices

The difference between a smoothie and a juice is that a smoothie contains the whole fruit and a juice contains just the juice of the fruit or vegetable. As a result a smoothie will contain more fibre and is the nutritional equivalent of eating the whole fruit. Fibre is important for good digestion and cardiovascular health. Smoothies are most often made from soft fruits such as strawberries, raspberries, blackberries, and grapes, which will easily blend to a puree. Juices can be made from hard fruits, including apples and pears, and vegetables. Juices do not contain the same fibre content as a smoothie, but a glass of juice can still be counted towards the recommended portions of fruit and vegetables per day.

Nutritional benefits

Juices and smoothies can help alleviate ailments, as well as help prevent illnesses, but don't wait until you feel below par to start enjoying the benefits of fresh fruit and vegetables. They are an important role in maintaining your general health.

Skin: Fruit and vegetables that are high in vitamin C help to build collagen, which is essential for general skin health. These include citrus fruit, strawberries, blackcurrants, peppers, and cabbage. Fruit and vegetables high in beta carotene such as apricots, carrots, squash, and spinach help protect the skin against sun damage. Vitamin E, which is found in nuts, seeds, dark green leafy vegetables, and wheat germ, helps protect against aging.

Hair and nails: Watercress, cucumber, and courgettes (zucchini) are good for healthy hair and nails.

Muscles and bones: Calcium is important for the healthy formation of bones and in the prevention of osteoporosis. It is found in milk and other dairy products, soy products, and broccoli. Vitamin K, found in leafy green vegetables, is also needed to maintain healthy bones.

Heart: Vitamin E, found in nuts, seeds, dark green leafy vegetables, and wheat germ, may help protect against heart disease. Garlic is also believed to be good for the heart. Fruit and vegetables high in beta carotene are required for a healthy heart too. Try apricots, dark leafy green vegetables, carrots, squash, and tomatoes.

Eyes: Choose fruit and vegetables high in beta carotene such as apricots, carrots, squash, blueberries, and spinach for good eye health. Vitamin C, found in many fruits and vegetables, is also known to help prevent the damage that leads to cataracts.

Stress: Grapes are good for their calming and restful qualities, as are oatmeal, celery, and chamomile. Foods that contain magnesium such as leafy green vegetables, nuts, and seeds will help reduce stress, as will those with the B vitamins (see page 11) and vitamin C. Try citrus fruit, berries, and peppers.

Energy: Pears, apples, bananas, and sweet potatoes are good for increasing energy levels. Orange and pineapple contain vitamin B_1, which is needed for energy production.

Detox: Fruit high in pectin or ellagic acid, including apples, strawberries, and grapes, are good for detoxing the body. Lemon and cranberry are good for the liver. Asparagus and garlic are good for cleaning the blood. Celery, cucumber, melon, and peaches have a diuretic effect and help prevent water retention. Cranberries and blueberries are good for the urinary tract.

Nausea and stomach problems: Ginger is a traditional remedy for nausea. Pineapple is good for the digestive tract, and fennel is great for digestion.

Immune system, colds, and flu: Include fruit and vegetables high in vitamin C and other antioxidants such as citrus fruit, berries – particularly dark red and purple berries such as blueberries and blackcurrants – peppers, spinach, and cherries. Broccoli and cabbage are believed to have cancer-preventing properties. Garlic and onions are good for colds, coughs, and flu.

Headaches: Fennel may help alleviate headaches. Cherries may have pain-relieving properties.

Vitamin and Mineral Sources

Although also present in other food sources, the following vitamins and minerals can be found in these fruit, vegetables, herbs and spices, dairy products, and nut and seed products used for making smoothies and juices.

Vitamins

A: Dairy products and dark green, orange, and yellow vegetables.

B$_1$: Cereals and nuts

B$_2$: Dairy products, broccoli, and spinach

Niacin: Cereals

B$_6$: Oats and peanuts

Folic acid (folate): Leafy green vegetables

B$_{12}$: Dairy products

C: Fruit and vegetables

E: Nuts, vegetables, and cereals

K: Leafy dark green vegetables

Minerals

Calcium: Dairy products and some vegetables

Magnesium: Nuts and seeds and green vegetables

Potassium: Nuts, onions, avocado, bananas and other fruit, and vegetables

Iron: Dark green vegetables and herbs

Zinc: Dairy products and cereals

Making Simple Juices

Some recipes for smoothies require the addition of fruit juices. You can use shop-bought juices, but if you have a juicer, you may want to make your own fresh juice for your smoothies, or you may simply want to make single fruit juices to drink. Here is a guide to how much juice you will get from the most popular fruit and vegetables.

To make 225ml/8floz/1 cup you will need:

Apple Juice: 4–5 apples
Orange Juice: 3–4 oranges
Pineapple Juice: ½ medium pineapple
Tomato Juice: 4–6 medium tomatoes
Carrot Juice: 5–6 large carrots
Grapefruit Juice: 2 grapefruit
Grape Juice: 225–300g/8–10oz/
   2–2½ cups grapes
Mango Juice: 1½–2 mangoes
Pear Juice: 4–5 pears
Cherry Juice: 450–500g/1lb–1lb2oz/
   2–2½ cups cherries
Pomegranate Juice: 4–5 pomegranates

Use these quantities only as a guide. These juices were made using a centrifugal juicer (see pages 16–17). If you use a masticating juicer, you will get a larger quantity of juice because these machines are more efficient. Also remember that the amount of juice will vary between the different varieties of the same fruit and even from season to season. Ripe local fruits in season are usually juicier than fruits that have been picked unripe and flown across the world.

Juices Hints and Tips

Recipes make one to two glasses, depending on the size of your glass and the amount you want to drink. In general, vegetable juices are drunk in smaller quantities than fruit juices.

Stick to one type of measuring system. Never switch between them. Cup measurements are for standard American cups.

Always use fruit and vegetables that are in peak condition.

Wash fruit and vegetables well before use.

Prepare fruit and vegetables just before you need them. Some vitamins will start to be destroyed when you cut into the produce, and some fruit and vegetables discolor quickly.

Use organic ingredients if you want to avoid pesticide residues.

Cut vegetables into pieces that can be fed through the juicer's feeding tube easily. This will vary from machine to machine. Some machines will take whole apples, others will need the fruit or vegetables to be cut up in small pieces.

Insert soft fruit such as strawberries and blueberries slowly to extract the most juice. Follow soft fruit and leaves with a harder fruit such as an apple or a vegetable.

If you do need to store the juice, keep it in the refrigerator and add a few drops of lemon juice. (This will keep it from discoloring.)

Serve well chilled – use chilled vegetables and fruit or serve over ice.

Dilute juices for children with an equal quantity of water. You can use sparkling mineral water to create a fizzy fruit drink.

Fruit is high in fructose, a natural sugar, so people with diabetes should not drink too much. Dilute with water if necessary.

Do not drink more than 3 glasses of juice a day unless you are used to it – too much juice can cause an upset stomach.

Very dark vegetables such as beetroot (beet) and broccoli can have strong flavors. Dilute with water or with a milder flavored juice such as apple or celery if you want.

Smoothie Bases

Many smoothies are 100 percent fruit, but to blend efficiently a liquid is often added.

Fruit juice: In 100 percent fruit smoothies, fruit juice is added if necessary. If you have a juicer, juice your own fruit to maximize the vitamin content (see pages 12–13). For speed or convenience, you can use shop-brought juices. Chilled juices not made from concentrate have the best flavor.

Yogurt: When yogurt is added as a base it adds valuable calcium to the smoothie. Using a yogurt with live bacteria is good for the digestion, providing healthy bacteria. Greek-style yogurt will give the creamiest results but has the highest calorie content. Whole-milk yogurt can be used as a substitute for Greek-style yogurt. It adds more creaminess to the drink than a low-fat yogurt, with a calorie content that is higher than low-fat yogurt but not as high as Greek-style yogurt. Fruit-flavored yogurt may have a lot of added sugar.

Milk: Like yogurt, milk added to smoothies provides a good source of calcium. Calcium is important for growing children, and smoothies are a good way of including milk in a fussy child's diet. Whole-fat milk has the most flavor, but for those wishing to reduce fat content, skimmed or semi-skimmed milk is better.

Cream: For special occasions, adding single (light) or double (heavy) cream to a smoothie will give it a richer flavor.

Crème fraîche, fromage frais, quark, cottage cheese, mascarpone: These dairy products can be added to smoothies to provide calcium and as thickeners. The fat content varies and those with a high-fat content such as full-fat crème fraîche and mascarpone should be used in moderation. Low-fat crème fraîche, cottage cheese, and fromage frais can be used more frequently. Cottage cheese and other low-fat cheeses also add protein and make a smoothie more filling. They are good additions when a smoothie is being served in place of a full meal.

Ice Cream and sorbet:
These can be added to smoothies for extra creaminess or flavor, as well as to to cool the drink. They can be blended with the fruit or added by the scoop in place of ice.

Dairy substitutes: Tofu is high in protein and low in fat. It is a good source of calcium and contains vitamin E. It has little flavor but will give your drink a more satisfying thickness and creamy texture.

Soy milk and soy yogurt can also be used as an alternative to dairy products, as can rice milk and oat milk. You can also use coconut milk, banana, and avocado to give smoothies a creamy texture and good flavor.

Smoothie Hints and Tips

Recipes make one to two glasses, depending on the size of your glass and the amount you want to drink.

Stick to one type of measuring system. Never switch between them. Cup measurements are for standard American cups.

Wash fruit and vegetables well. Peel if required and cut into chunks.

Use fruit and vegetables in peak condition.

Prepare fruit and vegetables just before you need them. Some vitamins start to be destroyed as you cut into the produce, and some produce discolors quickly.

Add liquids such as fruit juice, milk, or yogurt to the blender first.

For maximum nutritional benefit, serve the drinks immediately after preparing them.

Smoothies may separate on standing. This does not affect the flavor. Serve with a straw twizzler or spoon to stir before drinking.

Fresh ripe fruit should provide enough natural sweetness, but you can add a little extra sugar or honey to sweeten if required.

Keep berries and chopped up soft fruit such as apricots, peaches, and bananas in the freezer to make instant iced smoothies. They can go into the blender when frozen.

Smoothies are best served cold. Chill the ingredients before use and serve with plenty of ice. Crushed ice will cool a drink quickly. You can also use ice cream or sorbet.

Smoothies tend to be thick, but you can alter the thickness of the drink to your taste. Simply add extra milk, water, or fruit juice to achieve your preferred thickness.

If the smoothie is too thin, add a banana, which is a great thickener, or some frozen ingredients such as frozen fruit or ice cream. Or use cooked rice to thicken the smoothie.

You can remove seeds, pips, or fibrous material from the smoothie by straining through a nylon sieve. This will remove the fibre content, thus affecting the nutritional value of the drink, but it is useful if you find them unpleasant or you have fussy children.

Some liquids increase in volume and froth on blending so never overfill the blender.

Make sure the lid is firmly on your blender before processing.

Wash the blender as soon as possible after use. If fruit becomes dried on, soak in warm soapy water for a few minutes to soften the fruit.

Equipment

Whether you want to make juices, smoothies, or both, there is certain equipment that will be essential to have in your kitchen.

Juices

If you want to make juice from hard fruit and vegetables such as carrots, apples, and pears, you will need to invest in a juicer. There are two main types of juicers available.

Centrifugal juicer: This is the least expensive type and it works by finely grating the fruit or vegetables and then spinning them at high speed to separate the juice from the pulp, which is then discarded.

Masticating juicer: This machine is more efficient, but it comes with a higher price tag. It finely chops the fruit, then forces the juice out through a fine mesh.

Food processor: Some types have a centrifugal juicer attachment. It will not be as efficient as a dedicated machine; however, it will be more than adequate for occasional juicing.

Citrus juicer: Citrus juicer attachments are available for some juicers and food processors. These are specifically designed to squeeze juice from citrus fruit and are the most efficient equipment for juicing this kind of fruit. However, you can squeeze citrus fruit by simply peeling and feeding the segments through the juicers. Alternatively, you may prefer to use a simple hand lemon squeezer or reamer.

Smoothies

You may already have the equipment you need to make smoothies in your kitchen.

Blender: The best equipment for

making a smoothie is a blender, which consists of a jug placed on top of a motorized base, which powers the blades inside the jug. Use blenders for soft fruits such as strawberries and raspberries and always add some liquid to the jug.

Smoothie maker: This

specialized machine is a blender with a tap and nozzle at the base for easy pouring. It is not essential, but it will be a lot of fun and may encourage children to drink smoothies because they love to operate the tap.

Food processor: You can

use a food processor to make smoothies, although they generally tend to be less smooth. For the best results, add the fruit first and process before adding the liquid.

Electric wand:

This hand-held device will not be as efficient as a blender or food processor, but it is useful if you only make the occasional smoothie. You will need a deep bowl or jug for mixing.

Other Equipment

You will probably find most of the other equipment you require in your kitchen. Measuring jugs, cups, and spoons are useful to help ensure success every time.

You will need a chopping board and a sharp knife to prepare fruit and vegetables prior to juicing or making smoothies. For good hygiene practice, always use a separate board from one on which you prepare meat or fish.

A cherry stoner is useful if you want to make cherry juice.

A nylon sieve is useful to remove pips or seeds from smoothies or to make the smoothie thinner, but using one will remove some of the fibre from the juice.

2

Rise and Shine

Ruby Tuesday Pear Juice

2 pears, quartered
1 pomegranate
1 apple, quartered

1 Feed the pears through a juicer.

2 Cut the pomegranate in half and scoop out the flesh and seeds. Reserve a few seeds and feed the flesh and remaining seeds through the juicer.

3 Feed the apples through the juicer.

4 Pour into a glass and top with the reserved pomegranate seeds.

Long Ruby Tuesday Juice: Top up the juice with tonic, soda, or sparkling mineral water.

Spirulina, cholerella, and Klamath blue green algae, available

from health food shops, contain micronutrients and are sometimes referred to as super foods. They are a prefect addition to morning juices to give a real boost to your body's brain and nervous system.

Peach Divine

3 peaches, stoned
1 apple, quartered
1 banana, peeled
½ tsp spirulina, cholorella, or Klamath blue green algae (optional)

1 Place all the ingredients in a blender and blend until smooth.

2 Pour into a glass half-filled with ice.

Peach Divine II: Add 125ml/4floz/½ cup orange juice for a thinner smoothie.

Nectarine Divine: Replace the peaches with nectarines.

Super Veg Juice

1 red pepper, seeded and cut into strips
1 yellow pepper, seeded and cut into strips
Few spinach leaves
2 carrots, trimmed
3 sticks celery
¼ cucumber, peeled

1 Feed the vegetables in the order listed through a juicer.

2 Pour over ice in a glass.

Super Sweet Veg Juice: Add 1 peeled, cored, and seeded apple to feed through the juicer.

Carrots are packed with vitamin A, which will help your skin stay healthy.

Frozen Berry Smoothie

115g/4oz/1 cup frozen mixed berries, such as raspberries, blueberries, and blackberries
225ml/8floz/1 cup milk
4 tbsp whole-milk yogurt
1 tbsp icing (confectioners') sugar

1 Place all the ingredients in a blender and blend until smooth.

2 If the smoothies are too thick, stir in a little extra milk.

3 Pour into tall glasses to serve.

Black Forest Berries: Add stoned cherries to the frozen berry mixture (or choose a mixture with cherries).

Dairy-Free Berry Smoothie: Replace the milk with soy milk and yogurt with 50g/2oz/¼ cup silken tofu.

Berries are packed with **antioxidants**. Keep them in the freezer so you can enjoy their benefits any time of the year.

Spice 'n' Tropical

1 wedge pineapple, peeled and cut into chunks
½ small ripe mango, peeled, stoned, and cut into chunks
¼ papaya, peeled, seeded, and cut into chunks
1 small banana, peeled
Juice of ½ lime
Seeds of 3 cardamom pods, lightly crushed
Pinch ground chilli

1 Feed the prepared fruit through a juicer.

2 Stir in the cardamom and chilli, pour into glasses, and serve.

Amazake is made from fermented grains, which convert starches to simpler natural sugars. It can create a sweet creamy texture without added sugar or dairy products.

Amazing Amazake Smoothie

6 to 8 apricots, stoned
125g/4oz/½ cup brown rice amazake
4 tbsp orange juice

1 Place all the ingredients in a blender and blend until smooth.

2 Serve poured over ice.

Amazing Peach Amazake Smoothie:
Use 1 ripe peach instead of the apricots.

Amazing Raspberry Amazake Smoothie: Use 50g/2oz/½ cup raspberries in place of the apricots.

Muesli and Apple Smoothie

This smoothie is ideal if you run out of fresh fruit because it uses **nutritious dried fruit**. However, if you do have some fresh berries, add a few to the smoothie to make it even more healthy.

5 no-soak dried apricots, chopped
5 no-soak dried pitted prunes, chopped
4 tbsp no-added sugar and salt muesli
1 tbsp maple syrup
225ml/8floz/1 cup apple juice

1 Place all the ingredients in a blender.

2 Blend until smooth. Add a little extra apple juice if the smoothie is too thick for your liking.

Warm Muesli and Apple Smoothie:
Gently heat the apple juice until just simmering before adding to the blender.

Muesli and Milk Smoothie: Use milk in place of the apple juice.

Carrot and Apple Juice

2 large carrots, trimmed
2 apples, cut into wedges

1 Feed the carrots and apples through a juicer.

2 Pour into glasses and serve.

Carrot, Apple, and Celery Juice: Add 2 sticks of celery to the juicer.

night vision booster

Spicy Tomato Juice

8 large ripe tomatoes, quartered
2 carrots, trimmed
4 spring onions (scallions), trimmed
2.5cm/1 inch piece of ginger root,
   peeled
½ chilli, seeded
1 red pepper, seeded and cut into strips
4 sticks celery
Celery sticks to serve

1 Feed the vegetables in the order listed through a juicer.

2 Pour into glass and serve with celery sticks to stir.

Seedy Tomato Juice: Sprinkle a few mixed seeds such as sesame, pumkin, and sunflower seeds over the drink for extra nutritional benefits.

Easy Tropical

¼ small pineapple, peeled and cut into chunks
1 banana, peeled
125ml/4floz/½ cup apple and mango juice

1 Reserve a piece of pineapple and a slice of banana to decorate if desired. Place all the ingredients in a blender and blend until smooth.

2 Pour into a glass and decorate with the reserved fruit to serve.

Really Tropical: Add ¼ papaya, seeded and cut into chunks, to the blender.

Banana and Blueberry Yognog

1 banana, peeled
50g/2oz/½ cup blueberries
225ml/8floz/1 cup natural (plain) yogurt

1 Place all the ingredients in a blender and blend until smooth.

2 Pour into a glass and serve.

Banana and Raspberry Yognog: Use raspberries in place of blueberries.

Oatmeal releases energy slowly. Bananas have simple and complex carbohydrates and give instant energy without the blood sugar crash. This smoothie will keep you going until lunch time.

Banana and Oatmeal Smoothie

1 tbsp fine oatmeal
1 ripe banana
1 tsp clear honey
½ tsp vanilla essence (extract), optional
4 tbsp natural (plain) yogurt

1 Place the oatmeal in a blender and pour in 125ml/4floz/½ cup boiling water. Allow to stand for 10 minutes.

2 Reserve a slice of banana. Place the remainder in the blender with the rest of the ingredients and 125ml/4floz/½ cup cold water. Blend until smooth.

3 Pour into a glass and decorate with the banana slice.

Strawberry and Oatmeal Smoothie:
Add 115g/4oz/1 cup strawberries instead of the banana.

Mango Lassi

1 ripe mango, peeled, stoned, and cut
  into chunks
350ml/12floz/1½ cups whole-milk
  natural (plain) yogurt
Crushed ice

1 Place the mango and yogurt in a
  blender and whiz until smooth.

2 Pour over crushed ice in a glass
  to serve.

Banana Lassi: Replace the mango with
1 large, ripe peeled banana.

Spicy Lassi: Add ½ tsp ground
cinnamon and ¼ tsp grated nutmeg
to either the mango or banana lassi.

Banana and Coffee Morning Wake Up

1 ripe banana, peeled
125ml/4floz/½ cup strong hot coffee
125ml/4floz/½ cup hot milk

1 Place the banana in a blender with the coffee and blend until well combined.

2 Carefully add the hot milk and blend briefly to combine.

3 Pour into heat-proof glasses and serve.

Iced Banana and Coffee Wake Up:
Make the coffee and chill well. Proceed as above, adding a handful of ice to the blender with the banana and using chilled milk.

A meal in a glass is an ideal **substitute for breakfast**. The muesli provides quick and slow-release energy, the berries add valuable vitamins, and the yogurt and milk supply calcium.

Breakfast In a Glass

4 tbsp no-added sugar and salt muesli
1 tbsp maple syrup
Few blueberries
Few raspberries
225ml/8oz/1 cup natural (plain) yogurt
125ml/4floz/½ cup skimmed milk

1 Place all the ingredients in a blender and blend until smooth.

2 Pour into a glass and serve.

keep on moving

Pears are great **energizers** because instead of creating a suddern burst of energy, they release energy slowly.

Raspberry, Pear, and Almond Smoothie

2 pears, cut into wedges
1 orange, peeled and segmented
175g/6oz/1½ cups raspberries
4 tbsp ground almonds

1 Feed the pears and orange through a juicer and pour the juice into a blender.

2 Add the raspberries and ground almonds and blend until smooth.

Blackberry, Pear, and Almond Smoothie. Replace the raspberries with blackberries.

Strawberry, Pear, and Almond Smoothie: Replace the raspberries with strawberries.

Pear and Apricot Juice

2 pears, cut into wedges
1 apple, cut into wedges
6 apricots, stoned

1 Feed the fruit through a juicer.

2 Pour into a glass and serve immediately.

Apple and Apricot Juice: Instead of combining pears with an apple, use only apples – you'll need 3 apples.

Spinach and Pepper Punch

150g/5oz/3 cups baby spinach leaves
2 yellow peppers, seeded and cut into
  strips

1 Reserve a couple of strips of pepper.
  Feed the spinach and peppers through
  a juicer.

2 Pour into glasses and serve with the
  reserved sticks of pepper.

Creamy Spinach and Pepper Punch:
Stir the juice into 125ml/4floz/½ cup
natural (plain) yogurt.

This juice is power packed
with vital nutrients, making it a perfect
start to the day.

Strawberry and Vanilla Shake

115g/4oz/1 cup strawberries, washed
   and hulled
225ml/8floz/1 cup milk
4 tbsp vanilla-flavored yogurt
½ tsp vanilla essence (extract)

1 Reserve a strawberry to decorate. Place
all the ingredients in a blender and blend
until smooth. If the smoothie is too thick,
stir in a little extra milk.

2 Pour into a tall glass and decorate with
a strawberry to serve.

Raspberry and Vanilla Shake: Use
raspberries in place of the strawberries.

Blackberry and Vanilla Shake: Use
blackberries in place of the strawberries.

3

Liquid Lunch

Open Sesame Vegetable Juice

4 carrots, about 400g/14oz in weight
115g/4oz/¾ cup green beans (string beans), trimmed
1 tbsp tahini
Few toasted sesame seeds

1 Feed the carrots and beans through a juicer.

2 Stir in the tahini until well combined. If it is too thick, thin it with a little warm water before adding it to the juice.

3 Pour into glasses and sprinkle with sesame seeds.

Meal in One: If serving as a meal substitute, whisk in some soft tofu to provide protein.

Sesame seeds contain valuable nutrients, particularly calcium, which strengthens bones, as well as iron, vitamin E, and protein. Tahini is made from sesame seeds ground to a paste.

Winter Winner

1 large parsnip, trimmed
2 carrots, trimmed
Small handful coriander (cilantro)
1 small bulb fennel, cut into chunks
2 crisp green apples, quartered

1 Feed the parsnips and carrots through the juicer.

2 Feed the coriander (cilantro) through the juicer, followed by the fennel and apple.

3 Pour into glasses and serve.

Winter Winner Basilico: Use basil in place of the coriander.

Celery Winner: Replace the fennel with 4 or 5 sticks of celery.

keep yourself strong

Smokin' Red Pepper Juice

2 red peppers, seeded and cut
   into strips
1 large courgette (zucchini)
1 clove garlic
1 orange, peeled and segmented
½ tsp smoked paprika

1 Feed the pepper, courgette (zucchini), garlic, and orange segments through a juicer.

2 Stir in the smoked paprika and serve.

Sunny Smokin' Pepper Juice: Use yellow or orange peppers in place of the red pepper.

Rosy Smokin' Pepper Juice: Add 1 medium ripe tomato.

Totally Tropical Juice

½ mango, peeled and cut into chunks

¼ papaya, seeded, peeled, and cut
into chunks

1 wedge pineapple, peeled and cut
into chunks

1 kiwi fruit, peeled and cut
into wedges

1 banana, peeled

1 passion fruit

1–2 slices star fruit (optional)

1 Feed the first five fruits through
a juicer in the order listed.

2 Pour into a glass.

3 Cut the passion fruit in half,
scoop out the seeds, and stir
into the juice.

4 Decorate the glass with the star
fruit if desired.

Totally Tropical Smoothie: All the
fruit can be placed in a blender for
a super thick smoothie.

Carrot, Beetroot, and Ginger Juice

2 large carrots, trimmed
1cm/½ inch piece of ginger root, peeled
1 beetroot (beet), washed and trimmed

1 Feed the carrots, ginger, and then the beetroot (beet) through a juicer.

2 Serve well chilled.

Carrot, Beetroot, and Celery Juice:
Replace the ginger with 2 sticks of celery.

tame your tummy

Chilli Mango and Lime Smoothie

1 ripe mango, peeled, stoned and cut into chunks
2 limes
1 small red chilli, seeded and chopped
Few fresh mint leaves

1 Place the mango in a blender.

2 Squeeze the juice from the limes and add to the blender. Then add the chilli.

3 Blend until smooth.

4 Pour into a glass and top with a few small mint leaves.

Minty Mango and Lime Smoothie:
Replace the chilli with a few fresh mint leaves.

Waldorf Juice

4 sticks celery, cut into short lengths
2 tbsp raisins
1 tbsp walnuts
1 crisp apple, cut into wedges
1 tbsp low-fat fromage frais (yogurt) or
    crème fraîche (optional)
Celery sticks to stir

1 Feed the celery, raisins, walnuts, and
apple through the juicer.

2 Serve topped with the fromage frais
(yogurt) or crème fraîche and a
celery stick to stir.

Sweet Waldorf Juice: Add a carrot for
a slightly sweeter juice.

Cardamom is an aid to
digestion, and it is also thought
to help battle colds, fevers,
inflammatory conditions, and liver
problems. Ricotta cheese is a
good source of calcium.

Creamy Orange Delight

3 cardamom pods
115g/4oz/⅓ cup ricotta cheese
225ml/8floz/1 cup freshly squeezed
orange juice
1–2 tsp clear honey

1 Remove the seeds from the cardamom
pods and grind in a pestle and mortar.

2 Place in a blender with the ricotta
cheese and blend.

3 With the motor running, gradually pour in
the orange juice.

4 Sweeten with honey and serve over ice
if desired.

Pumpkin Pie Smoothie

150g/5oz/1¼ cups pumpkin flesh,
    cubed
¼ tsp ground cinnamon
Pinch grated nutmeg
1 small red chilli, seeded and chopped
225ml/8floz/1 cup orange juice

1 Steam the pumpkin for 10 minutes until just tender and let cool.

2 Place in a blender with the remaining ingredients. Blend until smooth.

3 Chill well and serve cold.

Spicy Squash Smoothie: Use a butternut squash instead of the pumpkin.

Cool Avocado Angel

1 avocado, peeled and stoned
½ cucumber, peeled and cut into
    chunks
225ml/8floz/1cup orange juice

1 Place all the ingredients in a blender and blend until smooth.

2 Pour into glasses half-filled with ice and serve.

Avocado Devil: Add 1 seeded, chopped red chilli to the mix to spice up the smoothie.

A super-charged avocado adds thickness to this smoothie. Avocado is an excellent source of potassium, folic acid (folate), and vitamin A, as well as protein, iron, and other vitamins and minerals.

sing from the heart

Deep Purple Smoothie

115g/4oz/¾ cup black or green grapes
115g/4oz/1 cup cherries, pitted
125ml/4floz/½ cup cranberry juice
Few cherries to serve

1 Feed the grapes through a juicer.

2 Add the grape juice, cherries, and cranberry juice to a blender and blend until smooth.

3 Pour over ice in glasses, decorate with a few cherries, and serve.

Nutty Banana Smoothie

1 banana
225ml/8floz/1 cup milk
1 tbsp smooth peanut butter

1 Peel and slice the banana, wrap it in clingfilm (plastic wrap), and freeze overnight.

2 Place all the ingredients in a blender and blend until smooth.

3 Pour in a glass and serve immediately.

Banana and Sesame Smoothie:
Instead of peanut butter use 2 tsp tahini.

Health in a Glass

2 medium tomatoes
210g/7½oz/3 cups cabbage,
   thickly shredded
Handful of parsley
Celery stick to serve

1 Feed the tomatoes, cabbage, and parsley through a juicer.

2 Pour into a glass and add a celery stick before serving.

Liquorice Liquor: Replace the parsley with 1 small bulb of fennel, cut into chunks.

Spinach is a good source of **folic acid** (folate), which is especially important for pregnant women. The tomatoes provide vitamin C, which helps to unlock the iron and calcium in spinach.

Green Giant Juice

2 medium tomatoes
150g/5oz/1¾ cups broccoli
150g/5oz/3 cups spinach

1 Cut a few slices from the tomato and reserve. Feed the tomatoes, broccoli, and spinach through a juicer.

2 Pour over ice in glasses and decorate with the tomato slices before serving.

Spiced Green Giant Juice: Add a pinch of grated nutmeg for some spice.

Strawberry and Mint Smoothie

115g/4oz/1 cup strawberries, washed
  and hulled
225ml/8floz/1 cup soy milk
85g/3oz/⅓ cup firm tofu
10 mint leaves, chopped
Mint leaves to decorate

1 Place all the strawberries, soy milk, and tofu in a blender. Add the chopped mint and blend until smooth. If the smoothies are too thick, stir in a little extra soy milk.

2 Pour into tall glasses and decorate with whole mint leaves to serve.

Raspberry and Mint Smoothie: Use raspberries instead of strawberries.

Blackberry and Mint Smoothie: Use blackberries instead of strawberries.

Creamy Borscht

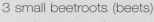

3 small beetroots (beets)
4 spring onions (scallions), trimmed
2 tsp lemon juice
85ml/3floz/¾ cup fromage frais (yogurt)
   or double (heavy) cream
Few chives, snipped

1 Feed the beetroots (beets) and onions (scallions) through a juicer.

2 Stir in the lemon juice and fromage frais (yogurt) or cream.

3 Pour into glasses and sprinkle with the snipped chives.

Borscht with a Kick: Add 1 tbsp dry sherry to the juice.

Slim 'n' Creamy Borscht: Use low-fat fromage frais or low-fat natural (plain) yogurt instead of the regular fromage frais or cream.

Beetroots (beets) are a good source of folic acid (folate) and vitamin C, and some people believe they have curative powers to relieve headaches and other aches and pains.

Banana Date Smoothie

125ml/4floz/½ cup milk

4 tbsp yogurt

1 tbsp date syrup

1 banana, peeled

4 dates, stoned and chopped

2 tsp wheat germ

1 Place all the ingredients in a blender and blend until smooth.

2 Pour into a glass and serve.

Dairy-free Banana Date Smoothie:
Use soy milk to replace the milk and yogurt for a dairy-free smoothie.

Wheat germ contains valuable B vitamins. Date syrup is a great way to add sweetness without adding sugar.

Gazpacho Smoothie

¼ red pepper
¼ green pepper
¼ red onion, peeled
¼ cucumber
1 clove garlic
Few sprigs parsley
1 tsp red wine vinegar
225ml/8floz/1 cup tomato juice
5 tbsp cold water
Dash Tabasco sauce
Freshly ground black pepper
Cucumber and parsley to decorate

1   Place all the ingredients in a blender and blend until smooth.

2   Serve chilled, decorated with slices of cucumber and a few parsley leaves.

The most colorful peppers provide the most bioflavonoids, which may help prevent cancer. Red peppers have more antioxidants than green peppers, but green peppers have more vitamin C than red peppers.

Lemongrass and Lime Smoothie

1 stick lemongrass
1 lime
2 tsp wheat germ
225ml/8floz/1cup whole-milk yogurt
1–2 tsp clear honey

1 Trim the ends of the lemon grass and remove the tough outer layers. Thinly slice the remainder; place in a blender.

2 Grate the zest from the lime and squeeze the juice. Add the zest and juice to the blender and blend until the lemon grass is finely chopped.

3 Add the wheat germ, yogurt, and honey and blend until smooth.

Lemongrass and Orange Smoothie: For a sweeter smoothie, replace the lime with 1 orange or 2 tangerines.

Peach and Almond Smoothie

2 peaches, stoned
2 tbsp toasted flaked almonds
225ml/8floz/1 cup freshly squeezed orange juice

1 Place the peaches and almonds in a blender and blend until smooth.

2 Add the orange juice and blend again.

3 Pour into glasses to serve.

Peach and Cashew Smoothie: Use lightly toasted cashew nuts instead of the almonds.

Peach and Hazelnut Smoothie: Use lightly toasted hazelnuts instead of the almonds.

 Wheat germ is packed full of calcium, and it has the B vitamins, vitamin E, magnesium, iron, and zinc, making this a nutritious ingredient.

Red Slaw Juice

½ small red cabbage, thickly shredded
1 carrot, trimmed
1 tbsp seedless raisins
2 apples, quartered
1 tbsp lemon juice

1 Feed the cabbage, carrot, raisins, and apples through a juicer.

2 Stir in the lemon juice and serve.

Nutty Slaw Juice: Grind a few shelled walnuts and add to the juice.

Fig and Apricot Smoothie

3 large figs, trimmed and quartered
4 apricots, stoned
1 tbsp wheat germ or oatmeal
125ml/4floz/½ cup freshly squeezed
   orange juice
1 tbsp lemon juice, freshly squeezed

1 Place all the ingredients in a blender and blend until smooth.

2 Pour into glasses and serve.

Fig and Date Smoothie: Replace the apricots with fresh pitted dates.

keep your tummy happy

Lime and Passion Fruit Cooler

1 lime
4 passion fruit
125ml/4floz/½ cup apple juice

1 Grate the zest from one lime and place in a blender. Cut the pith and peel away from the lime, then add the flesh to the blender.

2 Scoop out the passion fruit seeds into the blender, add the apple juice, and blend briefly.

3 Strain through a nylon sieve, pour into a glass, and serve.

Orange and Passion Fruit Cooler: Replace lime zest with orange zest and replace the apple juice with orange juice.

Tofu Cooler: Add 115g/4oz/½ cup silken tofu with the apple juice.

Carrot, Apple, and Ginger Juice

2 large carrots, trimmed and cut
  into chunks
2 apples, quartered
1cm/½ inch piece of ginger root, peeled
Carrot sticks to serve

1 Feed the carrot, apple, and ginger
  through a juicer.

2 Pour into glasses, add carrot sticks to
  stir, and serve.

Carrot, Apple, and Chilli Juice:
Replace the ginger with a small seeded
chilli for a real zip.

Ginger can help to relieve
nausea and morning sickness.

4

Sweet
Sensations

Coco-Nutty Peach Smoothie

2 peaches, stoned
225ml/8floz/1 cup canned coconut milk
½ tsp almond essence (extract)
50g/2oz/½ cup ratafia biscuits (almond-
    flavoured dried macaroons, similar to
    Amaretti biscuits), broken into pieces

1 Place the peaches, coconut milk,
almond essence (extract), and half the
biscuits in a blender; blend until smooth.

2 Pour into glasses and chill well.

3 Sprinkle the remaining biscuits on top
just before serving.

**Apricot, Almond, and Coconut
Smoothie:** Replace the peaches with
12 stoned apricots.

**Nectarine, Almond, and Coconut
Smoothie:** Use nectarines instead
of the peaches.

**Mango, Almond, and Coconut
Smoothie:** Use 1 peeled and stoned
mango instead of the peaches.

Ginger Cream Smoothie

2.5cm/1 inch piece of ginger root,
    peeled and grated
1 tbsp clear honey
125ml/4floz/½ cup natural (plain) yogurt
2 scoops vanilla ice cream

1 Place the ginger, honey, yogurt, and ice
cream in a blender; blend until smooth.

2 Serve immediately.

Choc 'n' Ginger Cream Smoothie:
Use 2 scoops of chocolate ice cream in
place of the vanilla ice cream.

Toffee 'n' Ginger Smoothie: Use
toffee-flavoured yogurt and toffee or
vanilla ice cream.

for a berry merry life

Tiramisu Smoothie

225g/8oz/1 cup mascarpone cheese
2–3 tbsp icing (confectioners') sugar
225ml/8oz/1 cup cold coffee
A little grated chocolate
Sponge fingers to serve

1 Place the mascarpone cheese, sugar, and coffee in a blender and blend until smooth, or whisk together in a bowl.

2 Pour into glasses and sprinkle a little grated chocolate on top.

3 Serve with the sponge fingers.

Warm Tiramisu Smoothie: Use hot coffee for a warm smoothie.

Strawberry Jam Shake

115g/4oz/1 cup strawberries, washed and hulled
2 tbsp strawberry jam
4 scoops strawberry ice cream
300ml/10floz/1¼ cups cold milk

1 Place the strawberries, jam, and two scoops of ice cream in a blender and blend until smooth.

2 With the machine running, gradually pour in the milk and blend until frothy.

3 Place a scoop of ice cream into each of two glasses and pour the milk shake over the ice cream.

Raspberry Jam Shake: Use fresh or frozen raspberries, raspberry jam, and raspberry ripple ice cream instead of the strawberry options.

Apricot Jam Shake: Use fresh apricots, apricot jam, and vanilla ice cream instead of the strawberry options.

Papaya and Coconut Cream

½ papaya, peeled, seeded, and cut
   into chunks
6–8 tbsp coconut milk
Juice of 1 lime

1 Place the papaya in a blender and
add the coconut milk and lime juice.

2 Blend until smooth. If too thick, add
a little extra coconut milk or water.

3 Pour into glasses to serve.

Mango and Coconut Cream: Replace
the papaya with mango.

Spicy Coconut Cream: Replace the
papaya with 2 peeled bananas and add
1 tsp mixed spice (allspice).

Iced Mocha Smoothie

2 tbsp cocoa powder
1 tbsp instant coffee granules
1 tbsp muscovado sugar (dark
   brown sugar)
350ml/12floz/1½ cups milk
4 tbsp single (light) or double (heavy)
   cream

1 Place the cocoa powder, coffee granules,
and sugar in a small heatproof bowl and
add about 4 tbsp boiling water. Stir until
the ingredients have dissolved.

2 Stir in the milk. Pour into a shallow
freezer container and freeze for about
2–4 hours until slushy.

3 Scoop into a blender, add the cream,
and blend to break up the ice crystals.
Serve immediately.

Iced Chocolate Smoothie: Omit the
coffee and stir the dissolved cocoa
powder and sugar into 50g/2oz melted
chocolate. Gradually whisk in the cold
milk and complete as above.

Spiced Coffee Granita

450ml/15floz/2 cups strong black coffee
4–6 tbsp demerara sugar (light
  brown sugar)
Grated zest of 1 orange
Pinch ground cloves
Pinch ground cinnamon
Pinch ground nutmeg
4 tbsp double (heavy) cream (optional)

1 Stir the sugar, most of the orange zest, and the spices into the freshly made black coffee and let cool.

2 Pour into a shallow freezer container and freeze for 2–4 hours until slushy.

3 Scoop into a blender, add the cream, and whiz to break up the ice crystals.

4 Serve immediately, with the reserved orange zest sprinkled on top.

Irish Coffee Granita: Add 2–3 tbsp Irish whiskey to the blender.

Brandied Coffee Granita: Add 2–3 tbsp brandy to the blender.

Pomegranate and Apple Juice

2 pomegranates
Few fresh mint leaves
4 crisp apples, quartered

1 Cut the pomegranates in half and scoop out the seeds.

2 Feed the seeds through a juicer, followed by the mint leaves and finally the apple.

Passion Fruit and Apple Juice:
Replace the pomegranate with 4 passion fruits.

Powerful antioxidants in the pomegranate may help prevent cancer and prevent hardening of the arteries. The seeds are an excellent source of fibre.

Pear and Choc Hazelnut Shake

1 soft ripe pear, peeled and cored
2 tbsp chocolate hazelnut spread or
    chocolate spread
225ml/8floz/1 cup milk
Vanilla or chocolate ice cream (optional)

1 Place the pear, chocolate hazelnut
spread, and milk in a blender and blend
until smooth and frothy.

2 Pour into glasses and add a scoop of
ice cream if desired.

Peach and Choc Hazelnut Shake:
Use one peach in place of the pear.

Banana and Choc Hazelnut Shake:
Replace the pear with a peeled banana.

Keep this for the occasional treat
because it has a high-fat content.
However, peanuts are a
good source of potassium and
folic acid (folate). Nuts are a rich
source of vitamin E, used to make
red blood cells.

Chocolate and Peanut Butter Shake

2 tbsp cocoa powder
50g/2oz plain (dark) chocolate, broken
    into chunks
2 tbsp smooth peanut butter
350ml/12floz/1½ cups milk

1 Place the cocoa powder in a heatproof
bowl with the chocolate, peanut butter,
and 3 tbsp of the milk.

2 Place over a pan of hot water and heat
gently, stirring until the chocolate melts
and the ingredients combine. Let cool.

3 Place in a blender and, with the motor
running, slowly add the remaining milk.

Choc-and-Peanut Ice Cream Shake:
Place a small scoop of chocolate ice
cream and one small scoop of vanilla
ice cream in the glasses and pour the
shake over the ice cream.

Rose and Strawberry Milk

15g/½oz scented rose petals,
    washed well, or 1 tbsp rosewater
300ml/10oz/1¼ cups milk
85g/3oz/¾ cup strawberries, washed
    and hulled

1 Place the rose petals in a small pan with half the milk and bring to a simmer. Remove from the heat and let cool. If you are using rosewater instead, simply add to the milk without heating.

2 Pour into a blender, add the strawberries, and blend until smooth.

3 Add the remaining milk and blend again. Chill before serving.

Rose and Raspberry Milk: Use raspberries in place of the strawberries.

Iced Coffee Shake

225ml/8floz/1 cup strong black coffee
2 tbsp demerara sugar (light brown
    sugar)
225ml/8floz/1 cup cold milk
4 tbsp single (light) or double (heavy)
    cream

1 Stir the sugar into a cup of freshly made black coffee and let cool.

2 Stir in the milk. Pour into a shallow freezer container and freeze for about 2–4 hours until slushy.

3 Scoop into a blender, add the cream, and blend to break up the ice crystals. Serve immediately.

Extra-Rich Iced Coffee Shake:
Add 2 scoops of vanilla ice cream to the blender.

make me feel happy

Berry Crush

Three or four 85g/3oz/¾ cup portions of:
  strawberries, blackberries, raspberries,
  blueberries, loganberries, bilberries,
  or cherries, pitted
125ml/4floz/½ cup orange or apple juice
1–2 scoops orange or lemon sorbet

1 Place your choice of fruit in a
   blender with the orange or apple
   juice and blend until smooth.

2 Pour into glasses and add a
   scoop of sorbet.

Creamy Berry Crush: Use
scoops of raspberry ripple ice
cream in place of the sorbet.

Green Goddess Smoothie

4 kiwi fruits, peeled and cut into wedges
115g/4oz/¾ cup gooseberries, trimmed
2–3 tbsp caster (superfine) sugar
   or clear honey
225ml/8floz/1 cup of milk or Greek-style
   natural (whole-milk plain) yogurt

1 Reserve a few slices of kiwi fruit to
   decorate. Place all the ingredients in a
   blender and blend until smooth.

2 Pour into glasses and float the reserved
   kiwi slices on top.

**Dairy-Free Gooseberry and Kiwi
Fool Smoothie:** Proceed as above,
replacing the milk or yogurt with either
soy milk or soy yogurt.

The fruit filled with immune-
boosting nutrients and milk or
yogurt loaded with calcium make this
a great health-boosting drink.

Melon, Apple, and Raspberry Smoothie

¼ wedge galia or honeydew melon, peeled
2 apples, quartered
115g/4oz/¾ cup raspberries

1 Feed the melon and apples through a juicer, then pour into a blender.

2 Add the raspberries and blend to combine.

3 Pour into a glass and serve.

Melon, Apple, and Strawberry Smoothie: Use strawberries in place of the raspberries.

make my heart beat happily

Plummy Apple Juice

8 ripe plums, stoned
2 apples, quartered

1 Feed the plums and apples through a juicer.

2 Pour into a glass and serve.

Plum, Apple, and Ginger Juice: Feed a 2.5cm/1 inch piece of peeled ginger root through the juicer after the plums.

Apricot and Apple Juice: Instead of plum use apricots. Add a 2.5cm/1 inch piece of peeled ginger root if desired.

Strawberry Ripple Smoothie

150g/5oz/1¼ cups strawberries, hulled
2 scoops vanilla ice cream
½ tsp vanilla essence (extract)
225ml/8floz/1 cup milk
50g/2oz meringue nests (or cookies),
   broken into small bite-size pieces

1 Place the strawberries in a blender with 2 tbsp water and blend to a purée, pour into a small bowl, and set aside.

2 Rinse out the blender. Place the ice cream, vanilla essence (extract), milk, and half the meringue nests in the blender and blend until smooth.

3 Pour alternate layers of strawberry purée, ice cream mixture, and meringue into the glasses. Finish with a few pieces of meringue on top.

Yogurt and Meringue Smoothie: Use vanilla yogurt in place of the ice cream.

Raspberry Ripple Smoothie: Use raspberries instead of strawberries.

Apple Custard Crumble

2 apples, peeled, cored, and sliced
225ml/8floz/1 cup ready-made custard
   (store-bought custard vanilla pudding)
125ml/4floz/½ cup milk
1 small granola bar, crumbled

1 Place the apples in a small pan with 4 tbsp water and cook over a low heat until soft. Allow to cool completely.

2 Spoon into a blender and add the custard, milk, and half the granola bar. Blend until well combined.

3 Pour into glasses and top with the remaining granola bar.

Rhubarb Custard Crumble: Replace the apples with 175g/6oz/¾ cup rhubarb cut into short lengths.

Blackberry and Apple Custard Crumble: Add 50g/2oz/⅓ cup blackberries to the blender.

Roo-Berry and Strawberry Smoothie

250g/9oz rhubarb, cut into 2.5cm/1 inch
   lengths
4 tbsp caster (superfine) sugar
115g/4oz/1 cup strawberries, washed
   and hulled
225ml/8floz/1 cup natural (plain) yogurt

1   Place the rhubarb, sugar, and 4 tbsp of
water in a small pan and cook gently for
10 minutes until softened.

2   Stir in the strawberries and remove from
the heat. Let cool.

3   Place in a blender with the yogurt and
blend until smooth.

4   Serve poured over ice.

Rhubarb and Raspberry Smoothie:
Use raspberries instead of strawberries.

Pineapple Colada Smoothie

½ small pineapple, peeled and cut into
   chunks
125ml/4floz/½ cup coconut milk

1   Reserve 1 or 2 pieces of pineapple to
decorate. Place the ingredients in a
blender and blend until smooth.

2   Pour into glasses and decorate with
reserved pineapple.

Pina Colada: Add a splash of rum and
some crushed ice for a pina colada.

Mango Colada Smoothie: Add the
flesh of ½ mango.

5

Bedtime
Soothers

Make a Date with Sleep Smoothie

1 banana, peeled
115g/4oz/½ cup amazake
4 fresh dates, stoned and chopped
125ml/4floz/½ cup milk or soy milk
Freshly grated nutmeg

1 Place the banana, amazake, and dates in a blender and blend until smooth.

2 Thin with milk or soy milk to your preferred consistency.

3 Sprinkle generously with nutmeg.

Dairy-Free Banana and Date Smoothie: Replace the milk with apple juice for a dairy-free alternative.

Banana and Raisin Smoothie: You can use 2 tbsp of seedless raisins instead of the dates.

Bananas contain the amino acid tryptophan, which helps you sleep, and nutmeg has phytochemicals, which also aid sleep.

Sleep Easy

1 tbsp fine oatmeal
80ml/2⅗floz/⅓ cup boiling water
90g/3½oz/1¾ cups iceberg lettuce
2 sticks celery
2 carrots

1 Place the oatmeal in a blender and pour the boiling water it. Let cool.

2 Feed the remaining ingredients through a juicer and stir into the oatmeal mixture.

Tomtato Sleep Easy: Replace the carrots with 1 large tomato.

Nutmeg has **calming** properties and the other spices help to give this drink a warming cosy spiciness. The oats will help to stave off any hunger pangs until morning.

Hot Choc Froth

350ml/12floz/1½ cups milk
1 tbsp cocoa powder
50g/2oz plain (dark) chocolate, broken into chunks
1 tbsp icing (confectioners') sugar
Few mini marshmallows

1 Place the milk in a small pan and heat until almost boiling.

2 Place the cocoa, chocolate, and sugar in a blender and carefully pour in half the hot milk. Blend until smooth.

3 Add the remaining milk and blend until frothy.

4 Pour into two heatproof glasses or mugs and top with marshmallows.

Almond Choc Froth: Add 25g/1oz Amaretti biscuits and ½ tsp almond essence (extract) if desired.

Hot & Spicy Apple Sleepy

2 apples, peeled, cored, and sliced
50g/2oz/¼ cup raisins
2 tbsp rolled oats
¼ tsp each ground cardamom, cinnamon, and nutmeg
Extra nutmeg to serve

1 Place the apples, raisins, oats, and 350ml/12floz/1½ cups of water into a small saucepan.

2 Bring to the boil, then reduce the heat and simmer gently for 5 minutes. Stir in the spices.

3 Let cool slightly, then carefully pour into a blender and blend at a low speed until smooth.

4 Pour into heatproof cups and sprinkle a little nutmeg over each drink before serving.

Chilled Spicy Apple Smoothie: Chill the apple smoothie and serve cold.

Banana Wind-Down Smoothie

Seeds of two cardamom pods
1 banana, peeled
225ml/8floz/1 cup freshly squeezed
   orange juice

1 Crush the cardamom seeds with a pestle and mortar; place in a blender.

2 Add the banana and orange juice, and blend until smooth.

3 Pour into a glass and serve.

Pineapple Wind-Down Smoothie:
Use a wedge of trimmed pineapple instead of the banana.

Chamomile is known for its **restful, soothing** qualities, and it also has anti-inflammatory and antispasmodic properties that can help to settle digestive problems.

Chamomile, Orange, and Elderflower Soother

1 chamomile teabag
1 orange
1 tbsp elderflower cordial

1 Place the teabag in a heatproof jug and cover with 225ml/8floz/1 cup of boiling water; let steep for 10 minutes.

2 Remove the teabag and discard.

3 Squeeze the juice from the orange and add to the tea. Add the elderflower cordial and stir.

4 Pour into a glass and serve immediately.

Chamomile, Orange, and Blackcurrant Soother: Use a blackcurrant cordial in place of the elderflower cordial.

get peeled and feel great

Grape Slumber Juice

225g/8oz/1 cup red or green grapes
2 oranges, peeled and segmented
1 tsp lemon juice

1 Feed the grapes through a juicer, followed by the orange segments.

2 Stir in the lemon juice and serve.

Brandied Grape and Orange Juice:
Add 2 tbsp brandy to the juice.

Oat-So-Sleepy Banana Smoothie

1 tbsp fine oatmeal
225ml/8floz/1 cup milk
50g/2oz/¼ cup seedless raisins
1 small ripe banana, peeled
1 tsp clear honey

1 Place the oatmeal in small pan with the milk and bring almost to the boil, stirring occasionally.

2 Carefully pour into a blender, add the remaining ingredients, and blend until the mixture is smooth.

3 Pour into a heatproof glass or mug and serve.

Dairy-Free Oat-So-Sleepy Smoothie:
Replace the milk with soy milk.

 Milk contains **tryptophan**, an essential amino acid that is a natural sleep inducer. If a skin forms over the milk, don't throw it away. Add it to the blender – the skin contains valuable nutrients.

Yogurt is full of **calcium** for healthy bones. Seeds add valuable good fats.

Honey Yogurt Flip

225ml/8floz/1 cup low-fat natural (plain) yogurt
2 tbsp clear honey
1 tbsp toasted mixed seeds such as pumpkin, sesame, and sunflower seeds
Ground cinnamon

1 Place the yogurt, honey, and half the seeds in a blender and blend briefly.

2 Pour into a glass and top with the remaining seeds. Sprinkle with cinnamon and serve.

Apple Honey Yogurt Flip: Add 1 peeled and cored apple to the blender.

Banana Honey Yogurt Flip: Add 1 small peeled banana to the blender.

Celery is known to have a calming restful effect and this juice should help to **promote sleep.**

Carrot and Celery Calmer

6 sticks celery, trimmed
4 carrots, trimmed
Carrot and celery sticks to serve

1 Feed the celery and carrots through a juicer and pour into glasses.

2 Serve with carrot and celery sticks.

Apple and Celery Calmer: Use 2 apples in place of the carrots.

6

Drinks for Dieters

Apple Power Booster

85g/3oz/¾ cup rocket (arugula) leaves
1 handful watercress
1 apple, quartered
1 stick celery, with its leaves

1 Feed the rocket (arugula) and watercress through a juicer, followed by the apple and celery.

2 Pour into glasses and serve.

Garlicky Apple Power: Omit the rocket and watercress, use 2 apples, and add 1 clove of peeled garlic.

Spinach Power Booster: Use spinach in place of the rocket.

Watercress is rich in antioxidants, which can help prevent cancer and some other diseases. Watercress is also a good source of vitamins A and C.

body-soothing king

Passionate Mango Smoothie

2 passion fruits
1 mango, stoned and peeled
125ml/4floz/½ cup low-fat natural (plain) yogurt
225/8floz/1 cup skimmed milk
Few ice cubes

1 Scoop the flesh and seeds out of the passion fruits and feed through a juicer with the mango.

2 Place the passion fruit and mango juice in a blender, along with the remaining ingredients, and blend until smooth.

3 Pour into a glass and serve.

Blackberry Delight

1 banana, peeled
115g/4oz/1 cup blackberries
175ml/6floz/¾ cup apple juice

1 Reserve 1 or 2 blackberries and 1 or 2 slices of banana to decorate. Place all the ingredients in a blender and blend until smooth.

2 Pour into tall glasses and decorate with the reserved fruit.

Raspberry Delight: Replace the blackberries with raspberries.

Raspberry and Orange Delight: Replace the blackberries with raspberries and use orange juice instead of the apple juice.

Basil and Orange Juice

4 oranges, peeled and segmented
Small handful basil leaves
Orange slice and basil leaves to serve

1 Feed half the oranges through a juicer, then add the basil leaves, followed by the remaining orange segments.

2 Pour into a glass and decorate with the orange slice and basil leaves.

Tomato and Basil Juice: Instead of the oranges, use 4 large or 6 medium ripe tomatoes. Feed half the tomatoes through the juicer, then add the basil, followed by the remaining tomatoes.

Orange and Parsley Juice: Use parsley in place of the basil.

Tomato and Parsley Juice: Use tomatoes and parsley and proceed as for Tomato and Basil Juice.

The beneficial volatile oils found in basil have antibacterial properties and can provide anti-inflammatory benefits. Basil is also a good source of beta carotene.

Carrot and Spinach Zing

6 carrots, trimmed
115g/4oz/1 cup spinach leaves
2.5cm/1 inch piece of ginger root,
    peeled
1 tsp Klamath blue green algae
    (optional)

1 Feed the carrots, spinach, and ginger through a juicer.

2 Stir in the Klamath blue green algae if using and serve over ice.

Carrot and Rocket Zing: Use rocket (arugula) in place of the spinach.

Carrot and Watercress Zing: Use watercress in place of the spinach.

Slimmer's Lassi

1 mango, stoned
225ml/8floz/1 cup low-fat natural
    (plain) yogurt
125ml/4floz/½ cup skimmed milk
Crushed ice

1 Place the mango, yogurt, and milk in a blender and blend until smooth.

2 Pour over crushed ice to serve.

Slimmer's Banana Lassi: Replace the mango with 1 large, ripe peeled banana.

Slimmer's Berry Lassi: Instead of the mango, use 115g/4oz/¾–1 cup of fresh berries.

Klamath blue green algae is packed with protein and minerals that are good for the body. It helps stop food cravings, which makes it ideal when dieting.

Cucumber is a good diuretic, so it can help stop water retention and aid weight loss. Cucumber also helps to lower blood pressure.

Melon and Cucumber Cooler

½ small honeydew melon, peeled, seeded, and cut into chunks
½ cucumber
Sparkling mineral water (optional)

1 Place the melon and cucumber in a blender and blend until smooth.

2 Pour into glasses.

3 Dilute with sparkling mineral water if required.

Melon, Cucumber, and Celery Cooler: Add 2 sticks of celery.

Watermelon and Orange Smoothie

450g/1lb/3 cups watermelon, peeled and cut into chunks
4 oranges

1 Discard most of the seeds and place the watermelon in a blender.

2 Squeeze the juice from the oranges and add to the blender.

3 Blend until smooth and serve over ice.

Watermelon and Lemon Smoothie: Instead of 4 oranges use 2 oranges and 2 lemons for a tangier flavor.

Melon and Orange Smoothie: Use honeydew, canteloupe, or another variety of melon instead of watermelon.

vitamin-packed

This is a fabulous low-cal drink that can be enjoyed any time of the day.

Watermelon and Ginger Refresher

450g/1lb/3 cups watermelon, peeled
    and cut into chunks
1cm/½ inch piece of ginger root, peeled
A little lemon juice
Sugar to taste

1 Feed the watermelon, followed by the ginger, through a juicer. Or blend in a blender, but grate the ginger first.

2 Pour into glasses and stir in a little lemon juice. Sweeten with a little sugar if required.

Melon and Ginger Refresher: Use a different variety of melon such as galia or honeydew melon.

Celery and Rocket Lift

2 sticks celery
Handful of rocket (arugula) leaves
225g/8oz/1 cup green grapes
Celery sticks to serve

1 Feed the ingredients through a juicer in the order listed.

2 Pour over crushed ice and add the celery sticks to stir.

Snappy Celery and Rocket Lift:
Add a few sugar snap pea pods after the grapes.

Pineapple is a good source for vitamin C and bromelain, which can help heal to wounds.

Summer Surprise

½ melon, seeded, peeled, and cut
   into chunks
½ pineapple, peeled and cut into chunks
1 mango, stoned and cut into chunks
115g/4oz/1 cup blueberries
1 tsp Klamath blue green algae
   (optional)

1 Place all the ingredients in a blender and blend until smooth.

2 Pour into glasses filled with plenty of ice.

Berry Surprise: Replace the blueberries, with strawberries, raspberries, or other berries of your choice.

Apricot and Prune Stand-By

6 pitted prunes, chopped
400g/14oz can apricots, in their juice

1 Place the ingredients in a blender and blend until smooth.

2 Serve over ice.

Peach and Prune Stand-By:
Replace the canned apricots with canned peaches.

Pear and Prune Stand-By: Use canned pears instead of the apricots.

Prunes are an appetite suppressant, so they are a perfect start to the day if you are watching the scales.

kung fu bad bacteria

Prune, Apple, and Pear Juice

12 prunes, pitted
2 apples, quartered
2 pears, quartered

1 Place the prunes in a heatproof bowl and cover with 125ml/4floz/½ cup boiling water. Let stand for 20 minutes.

2 Feed the apples through a juicer, followed by the soaked prunes and soaking water and then the pears.

3 Chill before serving.

Apricot, Apple, and Pear Juice: Replace the prunes with 8 stoned dried apricots.

Tomato Treat

8 medium tomatoes
Small handful fresh basil leaves
125ml/4floz/½ cup low-fat natural (plain) yogurt
115g/4oz/½ cup low-fat cottage cheese
1 tsp brewer's yeast, optional
2 sticks celery to serve

1 Place the tomatoes, basil, yogurt, cottage cheese, and brewer's yeast in a blender and blend until smooth.

2 Pour into glasses and serve with the celery sticks to stir.

Spicy Tomato Treat: Add ½ of a seeded red chilli for a little extra zing.

Salad Treat: Add ¼ of a cucumber, cut into chunks.

This low-calorie smoothie has **brewer's yeast**, a valuable vegetarian source for the B vitamins, iron, and zinc – all vital for a well-balanced diet.

Blackberry and Apple Juice

225g/8oz/1¾ cups blackberries
2 apples, cut into wedges

1 Reserve a few blackberries
and slices of apple for
decoration. Feed
the blackberries
and apples through
a juicer.

2 Pour into glasses
and decorate with
the reserved fruit.

**Raspberry and Apple
Juice:** Replace the
blackberries with
raspberries.

Cranberries can help prevent or alleviate cystitis and other urinary tract infections. They can also help prevent kidney and bladder stones.

Peachy Cranberry Fizz

115g/4oz/1 cup cranberries
1 tbsp caster (superfine) sugar
2 peaches, stoned
225ml/8floz/1 cup freshly squeezed orange juice
Clear honey or maple syrup, if desired
Sparkling mineral water to serve

1 Place the cranberries in a small pan with the sugar and 2 tbsp water. Cook for about 5 minutes until soft, then let cool.

2 Cut the peaches into pieces and place in a blender with the cranberries and orange juice. Add a little honey or maple syrup if you want a sweeter drink. Blend until smooth.

3 Strain through a nylon sieve, if desired, to remove the seeds.

4 Pour into glasses and top up with the mineral water.

Nectarine and Cranberry Fizz: Use nectarines in place of the peaches.

Plum and Cranberry Fizz: Use 8–12 plums in place of the peaches.

7

Body
Boosters

Pineapple and Papaya Power

½ pineapple, peeled and cut into chunks
½ papaya, peeled and cut into chunks
1 apple, quartered

1 Feed the fruit through a juicer.

2 Pour into glasses and serve immediately.

Pineapple Power Smoothie: Blend
the pineapple and papaya in a blender
with 125ml/4floz/½ cup orange juice.

Bromelain found in
pineapple reduces bruising so
if you have taken a knock or a
fall, try this juice to get you
back on your feet.

Nutty Bananas for the Muscles

1 medium banana, peeled
175ml/6floz/¾ cup soy milk
4 tbsp ground almonds
Few ice cubes
Cinnamon stick to serve

1 Place the banana, soy milk, ground
almond, and ice cubes in a blender.
Blend until smooth.

2 Pour into a glass and add a cinnamon
stick to stir.

bruise buster

This is a great detox juice. The Klamath has protein and minerals that will give your body a boost.

Cool Customer

4 apples, quartered
2 carrots, trimmed
1 stick celery
½ cucumber, peeled
1 tsp Klamath blue green algae (optional)
Cucumber slices to serve

1 Feed all the vegetables through a juicer and stir in the Klamath algae.

2 Pour over ice, decorate with cucumber slices, and serve.

Fruit and Cool: Replace the carrots with 2 pears for a fruity detox juice.

Pineapple Ginger Calmer

¼ pineapple, peeled
2.5cm/1 inch piece of ginger root, peeled
1 tbsp clear honey
Seeds of 4 cardamom pods, crushed
Strips of ginger stem or pinch of grated
   nutmeg to serve

1 Place all the ingredients in a blender
with 125ml/4 floz/½ cup of water. Blend
until smooth.

2 Thin the smoothie down to a desired
consistency with more water. If you have
an upset stomach, dilute the smoothie
and drink slowly.

3 Pour into a glass and decorate with the
strips of stem ginger or sprinkle with
nutmeg if desired.

Papaya Ginger Calmer: Use 1 papaya
in place of the pineapple.

For an upset stomach,
this drink contains pineapple,
which can help the digestive tract,
ginger, and cardamom, which can
relieve vomiting.

Citrus fruit such as grapefruit, oranges, lemons, and limes are loaded with **vitamin C**, which has an antihistaminic effect that can reduce the nasal symptoms associated with a cold.

Citrus Zing

1 grapefruit
3 oranges
1 lemon
1 lime

1 Juice the fruit: either cut in half and use a citrus juicer, or peel the fruit and feed the segments through a juicer.

2 Serve immediately for the maximum dose of Vitamin C.

Apple and Citrus Zing: If using a juicer, feed 2 crisp apples through the juicer after the citrus fruit.

Cherry and Orange Juice

Large handful of cherries, pitted
3 oranges, peeled and segmented

1 Feed the cherries through a juicer, followed by the orange segments.

2 Pour into a glass and serve.

Cherry and Orange Smoothie: Blend the cherries in a blender until smooth. Squeeze the oranges, add the juice to the blender, and whiz again.

It has been suggested that cherries have **painkilling properties**. One thing is for certain – they are packed with **pectin**, a fibre that can help lower cholesterol, and they are a good source of vitamin C.

love your life

Pineapple Energizer

1 pineapple, peeled, tough core
    removed, and cut into chunks
1 peach, stoned and cut into wedges
115g/4oz/1 cup strawberries, washed
    and hulled
Few blackcurrants
Freshly squeezed orange juice

1 Place the pineapple, strawberries, and
    currants in a blender with 125ml/4floz/
    ½ cup of orange juice; blend until smooth.

2 Add more orange juice to thin to your
    desired consistency and serve.

Blue Pineapple Energizer: Use
blueberries in place of the blackcurrants.

Creamy Carrot and Cardamom Dream

6 carrots, trimmed
4 tbsp single (light) cream, low-fat
    fromage frais (yogurt), or quark
Seeds of 4 cardamom pods, crushed

1 Feed the carrots through a juicer.

2 Stir in the cream, fromage frais (yogurt),
    or quark; add the cardamom seeds.

3 Pour into a glass to serve.

Creamy Carrot and Coriander Dream: Replace the cardamom with a
small handful of coriander leaves
(cilantro) and feed through the juicer.

Creamy Carrot and Parsley Dream:
Replace the cardamom with a handful of
parsley and feed through the juicer.

Carrots are rich in beta carotene and are good for
the immune system, skin, and
eyes. Cardamom is thought to
help fight colds and fever.

live life to the full

Raspberry and Banana Tofu Smoothie

115g/4oz/1cup raspberries
1 small banana, peeled
175g/6oz/¾ cup soft tofu
350ml/12floz/1½ cups freshly squeezed
    orange juice

1 Place the raspberries, banana, and tofu in a blender and blend until smooth.

2 Add the orange juice and blend again.

3 Pour into glasses and serve.

Strawberry and Banana Tofu Smoothie: Replace the raspberries with strawberries.

Blackberry and Banana Tofu Smoothie: Use blackberries instead of raspberries.

Tofu, a good all-round food, is high in protein, calcium, and vitamin E, and low in saturated fats, making it great for strong muscles and bones.

Fruity Beety Beauty

2 beetroots (beets), trimmed
1 large orange, peeled
Small handful fresh raspberries

1 Cut the beetroots (beets) into quarters and feed half through a juicer.

2 Next feed the orange segments through, then the remaining beetroots (beets). Pour the juice into a blender.

3 Add the raspberries to the blender and blend until smooth.

4 Pour into a glass and serve.

Enjoy this juice to boost your immunity. Beetroot is a good source of folate and vitamin C.

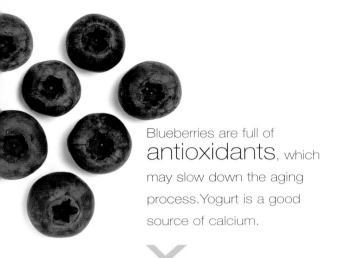

Blueberries are full of **antioxidants**, which may slow down the aging process. Yogurt is a good source of calcium.

Blueberry Yog Nog

115g/4oz/1 cup blueberries
225ml/8floz/1cup low-fat natural
   (plain) yogurt
1 tbsp clear honey
1 tbsp sunflower seeds

1 Place the blueberries, yogurt, and honey in a blender and blend until smooth.

2 Pour into glasses and sprinkle with the sunflower seeds.

Raspberry Yog Nog: Use raspberries in place of the blueberries.

Yog Nog with Pumpkin Seeds: Use pumpkin seeds instead of sunflower seeds.

Passion Zoom

1 small mango, peeled, stoned, and
   cut into chunks
1 wedge pineapple, peeled and cut
   into chunks
12fml/4floz/½ cup orange juice
1 passion fruit

1 Place the mango, pineapple, and orange juice in a blender and blend until smooth.

2 Cut the passion fruit in half and scoop out the seeds. Add to the blender and blend briefly.

3 Pour over ice and serve.

Creamy Passion Zoom: Replace the pineapple with a peeled banana.

This refreshing juice is packed full of antioxidants that are perfect for building up your **immune system**.

Grapes and berries contain sulphur, which is good for **healthy skin**.

Grape and Raspberry Glow

225ml/8floz/1cup red grape juice
175g/6oz/1½ cups raspberries

1 Place the fruit in a blender, reserving a few raspberries. Blend until well combined.

2 Push through a nylon sieve to remove seeds if desired.

3 Pour into a glass and top with reserved raspberries.

Green Grapes and Blueberry Glow: Substitute the ingredients with seedless green grapes and blueberries.

Pineapple has one of the strongest protein-digesting enzymes, bromelain, and melons have diuretic and digestive cleansing properties, making this drink ideal for improving your digestive system and helping to alleviate digestive problems.

Melon, Pineapple, and Mango Smoothie

1 wedge cantaloupe melon, peeled and cut into chunks
1 wedge pineapple, peeled and cut into chunks
½ mango, peeled and cut into chunks
125ml/4floz/½ cup freshly squeezed orange juice
Mango slices to decorate

1 Place all the ingredients in a blender and blend until smooth.

2 Pour over ice, if desired, and decorate with slices of mango.

Fruity Juice: Feed the ingredients through a juicer for a thinner juice drink.

Papaya, Pineapple, and Mango Smoothie: Give the drink even more protein-digesting enzymes by adding a wedge of papaya to the mix.

Minty Tummy Calmer

225g/8oz/2 cups strawberries, hulled
1 lime
2 tbsp freshly chopped mint
1–2 tbsp clear honey or maple syrup
   (optional)

1 Feed the strawberries through a juicer.

2 Squeeze the juice from the lime and
   stir into the strawberry juice.

3 Stir in the chopped mint. Sweeten with
   a little honey or maple syrup if desired.

4 Pour into a glass and serve.

Strawberry Tummy Calmer: Add the
juice of 1 lemon instead of lime.

Strawberry and Black Pepper Juice

350g/12oz /1½ cups strawberries,
   washed and hulled
2 apples, quartered
¼ tsp crushed black pepper

1 Feed the strawberries and apples
   through a juicer.

2 Stir in the pepper and serve.

Strawberry and Balsamic Juice: Add
½ tsp balsamic vinegar with the pepper
for a fabulous tang.

Strawberries contain the
phytochemical ellagic
acid, which is believed to help
prevent cancer, making this sweet
juice a healthy choice.

Fennel and carrot juice creates a popular combination that has been used for centuries as a traditional remedy for poor eyesight. This combination is also used to help relieve headaches and may help menopausal or menstrual problems too.

Bright-Eyed Woman

1 fennel bulb, trimmed
3 carrots, trimmed

1 Feed the fennel and carrots through a juicer.

2 Pour into a glass and add ice if required.

Sprouty Bright-Eyed Woman: Add a handful of alfalfa sprouts, which are high in vitamins A, C, and K.

Green Bright-Eyed Woman: Add 1 carrot and ½ an avocado – it is high in vitamin E, which is good for healthy skin.

Berry Booster

Three or four 85g/3oz/¾ cup portions of: strawberries, blackberries, raspberries, blueberries, loganberries, bilberries, or cherries, pitted
A little clear honey (optional)

1 Feed the berries of your choice through a juicer.

2 Sweeten with a little honey if desired.

Berry and Orange Booster: Substitute one portion of berries with 125ml/4floz/½ cup fresh orange juice.

pack a healthy punch

Carrot, Parsnip, and Avocado Blemish Blaster

2 large carrots, trimmed
1 parsnip, trimmed and cut into chunks
1 avocado, peeled and stoned
½ lemon

1 Feed the carrots and parsnips through a juicer.

2 Place the avocado in a blender, then add the carrot, parsnip, and lemon juices. Blend until smooth.

3 Pour into a glass and serve.

Carrot, Apple, and Avocado Smoothie: Use 2 carrots, 1 apple, and the avocado.

This is a good healing juice for people with acne or other skin complaints. The smoothie is high in vitamin E, which is important for healthy skin.

Apple and melons are both great for **detoxing** the body.

Melon, Blackberry, and Apple Detox

¼ wedge galia or honeydew melon,
   peeled
115g/4oz/1 cup blackberries, washed
   and hulled
175ml/6 floz/¾ cup apple juice

1 Place the melon and blackberries in a
blender with the apple juice and blend
until smooth.

2 Pour over ice if desired and serve.

**Melon, Raspberry, and Apple
Smoothie:** Replace the blackberries
with raspberries for a lighter smoothie.

say bye-bye to muscle aches

Rosemary Red

200g/7oz/1½ cups raspberries
115g/4oz/1 cup redcurrants
115g/4oz/1 cup blackcurrants
125ml/4floz/½ cup orange or grape juice
1 tsp freshly chopped rosemary

1 Place all the ingredients in a blender and blend until smooth. If desired push through a nylon sieve to remove seeds.

2 Pour into glasses and serve.

Ginger Red: Add 2.5cm/1 inch piece of peeled and grated ginger root in place of the rosemary.

Tarragon Red: Use tarragon in place of rosemary.

Berries are good sources of **proanthocyanins** and vitamin C, which are required for a healthy immune system. They may also have properties that protect against cancer.

Cold Buster

2 kiwi fruits, peeled and cut into wedges
2 apples, cut into wedges
2 tbsp lemon juice
1 tsp echinacea (optional)

1 Feed the fruit through a juicer.

2 Stir in the lemon juice and echinacea; serve immediately.

Pear Cold Buster: Replace the apples with pears.

Echinacea (available from health food shops) helps relieve the symptoms of colds and flu. The antiseptic properties found in lemon juice are also good for fighting off colds.

Apricot Hormone Juice

225ml/8floz/1 cup soy milk
3 tbsp probiotic yogurt
1tsp tahini
6 apricots, stoned
Few toasted sesame seeds

1 Place the milk, yogurt, tahini, and apricots in a blender and blend until smooth.

2 Pour into glasses, sprinkle the sesame seeds on top, and serve.

Peach Hormone Juice: Use 1 peach in place of the apricots.

This juice is high in calcium and the apricots provide potassium. This drink has a balancing effect that may help when hormones are affecting your mood.

The sour flavor of the gooseberries is counteracted by the sweetness of the kiwi fruits in this immune-boosting juice, which is a good source of vitamin C, potassium, and bioflavonoids.

Gooseberry and Kiwi Juice

6 kiwi fruits, cut into wedges
150g/5oz/1 cup gooseberries
1 sweet apple, quartered

1 Feed the ingredients through a juicer.

2 Pour into a glass and serve.

Gooseberry, Pear, and Kiwi Juice: Omit the apple and use 4 kiwi fruits and 2 quartered pears.

8

Power
Potions

Sweet Potato and Cabbage Energizer

2 carrots, trimmed
1 small sweet potato, peeled and cut
   into chunks
½ small savoy cabbage, shredded
Handful of seaweed
2 tsp sesame seeds

1 Place the carrots, sweet potato, cabbage, and seaweed in a blender and blend until smooth.

2 Pour into glasses, sprinkle the sesame seeds on top, and serve.

Oriental Energizer: Replace the cabbage with ½ medium head of Chinese cabbage and add a handful of pak choy.

Seaweed is a rich source of minerals and the sesame seeds are an excellent source of energy, making this combination a good drink for anyone who is experiencing stress and fatigue.

This energizing drink is the perfect boost when coping with a **work overload**. It's packed with vitamins A, C, and E and potassium and will help you to improve your mental capacity to concentrate.

Rocket Booster

2 carrots, trimmed
1 kiwi fruit
1 large tomato
Handful of rocket (arugula)
Handful of watercress
2 apples, quartered

1 Cut two slices from a tomato and reserve. Feed the remaining ingredients through a juicer.

2 Pour into glasses, decorate with the tomato slices, and serve.

Spinach Booster: Replace the rocket (arugula) with a handful of spinach.

Juicy Joints

½ mango, peeled and stoned
1 banana, peeled
1 apple, quartered
1 pear, quartered
225g/8oz/2 cups strawberries, washed
  and hulled
2 tsp tahini

1 Reserve a strawberry and a couple of slices of banana. Feed the remaining fruit through a juicer.

2 Dilute the tahini with a little hot water if required and stir into the juice.

3 Pour into glasses and decorate with reserved fruit.

Juicy Blueberry: Replace the strawberries with blueberries.

This vitamin-packed drink will help keep your muscles going through the day. Mangoes are a rich source of beta carotene, potassium, and iron. They are also high in pectin, a fibre that can help to control blood cholesterol.

Packed with **protein** and calcium, this is a great shake for those who want to build body weight rather than reduce it. Muscles weigh more than fat.

Muscle Magic

1 banana, peeled
½ papaya, peeled and seeded
115g/4oz/½ cup silken tofu
225ml/8floz/1 cup whole-milk natural
    (plain) yogurt
1 tsp wheat germ
Slices papaya to serve

1 Place all the ingredients, except the slices of papaya, in a blender and blend to combine.

2 Pour into glasses, decorate with the papaya slices, and serve immediately.

Dairy-Free Muscle Magic: Use a soy yogurt instead of a dairy yogurt.

A perfect drink for before or after **exercise**, wheat germ has the B vitamins, vitamin E, proteins, and minerals. Linseeds have essential fatty acids (good oils), and banana and avocado are good for supplying energy.

Easy Exerciser

2 tbsp wheat germ
1 small banana, peeled
½ avocado, peeled and stoned
125g/4oz/½ cup natural (plain) yogurt
1 tbsp linseeds
2 tbsp lime juice
6 tbsp orange juice

1 Place all the ingredients in a blender and blend until well combined.

2 Pour into a glass and sprinkle with a few more linseeds if desired.

Banana Exerciser: Replace the avocado with ½ of a peeled banana.

Hearty Red Pepper and Sweet Potato

2 red peppers, seeded and cut
    into strips
1 clove garlic
Few basil leaves
1 medium sweet potato, peeled and
    cut into chunks
2 carrots

1 Feed the vegetables in the order listed through a juicer.

2 Pour over ice and serve.

Hearty Yellow Pepper and Sweet Potato: Use yellow peppers instead of the red peppers.

Hearty Green Pepper and Sweet Potato: For a slightly sharper juice, use green peppers instead of red peppers.

Sweet potatoes are a rich source of **beta carotene**, which can be converted to vitamin A in the body. They are also packed with vitamin C and potassium. Garlic is good for the **heart**.

stand tall and strong

Broccoli has almost as much **calcium** as milk, so this juice is ideal for boosting calcium levels in people on a dairy-free diet. Calcium is an essential aid for women in helping to prevent osteoporosis.

Calcium Booster

175g/6oz/1 cup broccoli florets
2 crisp apples, quartered
1 tbsp lime or lemon juice

1 Feed the broccoli and apples through a juicer and stir in the lime juice.

2 Pour into a glass and serve.

Creamy Calcium Booster: Boost the calcium content further by adding 2 tbsp natural (plain) yogurt.

Love your Heart

½ cucumber, peeled
1 avocado, peeled and stoned
Celery stick to stir

1 Feed the cucumber through a juicer.

2 Place the juice and the avocado in a blender and blend until smooth.

3 Pour into a glass, add the celery stick, and serve immediately.

Cucumber can help **lower blood pressure**.
As well as being important for cardiovascular health, the avocado may also help to keep you looking good – it is packed with vitamin E, which is good for the skin.

Purple Power

½ small red cabbage, thickly shredded
2 pears, quartered
1 tbsp lemon juice

1 Feed the cabbage and pears through a juicer. Stir in the lemon juice.

2 Pour into glasses and serve.

Fennel Power: Feed ½ a trimmed fennel bulb through the juicer after the pears.

Pears are a great energizer, and they are combined here with red cabbage for a great tasting power juice. Cabbage is loaded with vitamin C, especially red cabbage, and may help prevent colon cancer.

With plenty of the B vitamins, this juice is sure to boost your brain power.

Memory Master

2 fresh dates, stoned and chopped
4 dried apricots, stoned and chopped
2 tbsp seedless raisins
225ml/8floz/1 cup natural (plain) yogurt
1–2 tsp brewer's yeast

1 Place the dates, apricots, and raisins in a blender with 6 tbsp water and purée until smooth.

2 Add the yogurt and brewer's yeast and blend again.

3 Pour into a glass and serve.

Wheat Master: Replace the brewer's yeast with wheat germ.

Pineapple is a good source of thiamine, riboflavin, and manganese, and these are all important for energy production.

On the Go

½ pineapple, peeled and cut into chunks
1 large banana, peeled
115g/4oz/1 cup strawberries, washed and hulled

1 Place all the ingredients in a blender and blend until smooth.

2 Pour into glasses and serve.

Stay On the Go: Add to the blender a little cooked brown rice for slow-released energy. Thin with a little water or apple juice if desired.

Sunny Tofu Smoothie

225g/8oz/1 cup soft tofu
225g/8oz/2 cups mixed berries such as blackberries, raspberries, strawberries, and red or blackcurrants
1 tbsp lime juice
Pineapple juice
1 tbsp sunflower seeds

1 Place the tofu, berries, lime juice, and a splash of pineapple juice in a blender and blend until smooth.

2 Add extra pineapple juice until you have a smoothie of your preferred thickness.

3 Pour into glasses and sprinkle with sunflower seeds to serve.

Orange Tofu Smoothie: Use orange juice in place of the pineapple juice.

Tofu, made from soy beans, is a great vegetarian source of protein and iron, and it has the B vitamins, calcium, potassium, and other minerals, making it an energizing drink.

Try this smoothie for a stress-free start to the day. Avocado contains oleic acid, which is good for the heart. Bananas, which are a rich source of potassium, are good for lowering blood pressure.

Heart Pacer

1 small banana, peeled
1 small avocado, peeled and stoned
1 tbsp clear honey
225ml/8floz/1 cup soy milk
Few raspberries

1 Place the banana and avocado in a blender and blend until smooth.

2 Add the honey and milk; blend again.

3 Pour into glasses and top with a few fresh raspberries.

Heart Pacer with Dates: For an even greater dose of potassium, add a few chopped dates to the blender in step 1.

Blueberry Heart Pacer: Top with a handful of blueberries in place of the raspberries.

Green Surprise

115g/4oz/½ cup broccoli florets
Small handful watercress
Small handful parsley
½ pineapple, peeled and cut into chunks
½–1 tsp spirulina, chlorella, or Klamath blue green algae (optional)

1 Feed the broccoli, watercress, and parsley through a juicer. Follow with the pineapple.

2 Stir in the spirulina, chlorella, or Klamath blue green algae if using.

3 Pour into glasses and serve.

Popeye Surprise: Use spinach instead of the watercress.

This vitality juice will give you strength and energy you never knew you had. Watercress, as well as being good for the hair and nails, has a good supply of iron, magnesium, and calcium. Spirulina, chlorella, and Klamath contain minerals that are often missing from our daily diet.

Red Berry and Willing

115g/4oz/1 cup strawberries, washed
  and hulled
115g/4oz/1 cup blueberries
1 tsp ginseng powder (optional)
2.5cm/1 inch piece of ginger root,
  peeled
1 tbsp clear honey
125ml/4floz/½ cup freshly squeezed
  orange juice

1 Reserve a strawberry and a few
  blueberries. Place all the ingredients in
  a blender and blend until smooth.

2 Pour into glasses, decorate with the
  reserved fruit, and serve.

Currants, Berry, and Willing: Add
some redcurrants and blackcurrants for
a super fruity smoothie.

Blueberries are a good source of zinc
and other nutrients that can give a
boost to the **reproductive
hormones** of both men and
women. Strawberries have long been
thought of as the fruit of love.

Broccoli, carrots, and cucumber are good sources of ZINC, which is vital for healthy sperm.

One for the Men

4 carrots, trimmed
85g/3oz/⅓ cup broccoli florets
¼ cucumber, peeled
4 tbsp ground almonds
1 tsp pumpkin seeds
1 tsp sunflower seeds

1 Feed the carrots, broccoli, and cucumber through a juicer.

2 Stir in the ground almonds.

3 Pour into glasses, sprinkle the seeds on top, and serve.

Another for the Men: Replace the broccoli with a handful of watercress.

9

Alcoholic Juices and Smoothies

Watermelon Blast

1 small watermelon, chilled
225ml/8floz/1 cup white grape juice
Juice of 1 lime
85ml/3floz/⅓ cup white rum
Sugar to taste
Crushed ice

1 Cut the watermelon into slices. Reserve one slice for garnish. Remove the rind and seeds from the other slices, and chop the flesh into chunks.

2 Place the watermelon flesh into a blender. Add the grape juice, lime juice, and rum. Add sugar to taste and blend until smooth.

3 Fill two glasses with crushed ice and pour the watermelon cocktail over it. Garnish with the watermelon slices.

Orange Blast: Replace the watermelon with a ripe cantaloupe and the grape juice with orange juice.

Kiwi Daiquiri

60ml/2floz/¼ cup white rum
2 tbsp fresh lime juice
3 ripe kiwi fruits, peeled and
   cut into chunks
Crushed ice
Kiwi slices to serve
Mint sprig to serve

1 Place the rum, lime juice, kiwi chunks, and ice into a blender. Blend at slow speed for 5 seconds, then at high speed for 20 seconds.

2 Pour into chilled glasses and decorate with kiwi slices and mint sprigs.

Strawberry Daiquiri: Replace the kiwi fruits with 8 large, ripe strawberries and blend at slow speed.

Pear and Aniseed

3 pears, cut into wedges
2 apples, cut into wedges
3–4 tbsp pernod
Crushed ice

1 Feed the pears and apples through a juicer.

2 Stir in the pernod and pour over crushed ice divided between two glasses to serve.

Pear and Brandy: Use brandy or calvados in place of the pernod.

Gingered Apple Fizz

2 apples, cut into wedges
1cm/½ inch piece of root ginger, peeled
60ml/2floz/¼ cup apple brandy
Sparkling water

1 Feed the apples and ginger through a juicer and pour into glasses.

2 Stir in the apple brandy and top up with sparkling water.

Gingered Pear Fizz: Replace the apple with pears.

face life with a smile

Cranberry and Orange Punch

115g/4oz/1 cup cranberries
125ml/4floz/½ cup orange juice
2 tbsp muscovado sugar (dark
 brown sugar)
125ml/4floz/½ cup red wine
2 cinnamon sticks

1 Place the cranberries, orange juice, and sugar in a saucepan and cook for 10 minutes until the cranberries are soft.

2 Let cool slightly, then blend in a blender until smooth.

3 Return to the pan and heat gently. Stir in the wine and heat until only just simmering.

4 Pour into glasses and serve with a cinnamon stick stirrer.

Non-Alcoholic Cranberry Punch:
Substitute red grape juice for the wine.

Bellini

1 peach, stoned
225ml/8floz/1 cup chilled champagne

1 Place the peach into a blender and blend until smooth.

2 Pour into two glasses and gradually top up with champagne.

3 Serve with a twizzler to stir.

Strawberry Bellini: Omit the peaches and blend 8 medium strawberries in the blender and complete as above.

Citrus Vodka Cocktail

Ice
4 tbsp vodka
4 tbsp freshly squeezed
  grapefruit juice
1 tbsp orange-flavored liqueur
1 tbsp grenadine
Orange slices to serve

1 Place a handful of ice in a blender and pour in the vodka, grapefruit juice, and orange liqueur.

2 Blend for a few seconds until the ice is crushed.

3 Pour into glasses and carefully pour a little grenadine down the side of the glass, decorate with the orange slices, and serve.

Citrus Gin Cocktail: Use gin in place of the vodka.

Orange Vodka Cocktail: Replace the grapefruit juice with freshly squeezed orange juice.

Lime juice is a good source of vitamin C. Without this vitamin your body cannot produce collagen, a fibrous substance that holds cells together.

Frozen Lemon Daiquiri

6 tbsp white rum
1 tsp fresh lime juice
1 tbsp freshly squeezed orange juice
2 scoops lemon sorbet
Few fresh raspberries

1 Place the rum, lime juice, orange juice, and sorbet in a blender and blend until smooth.

2 Pour into two glasses and float a few fresh raspberries on top of each.

Strawberry Daiquiri: Replace the sorbet with strawberry sorbet and decorate with fresh strawberry slices.

Orange Daiquiri: Use orange sorbet and decorate with fresh raspberries or redcurrants.

Bloody Mary

8 large ripe tomatoes, quartered
4 spring onions (scallions), trimmed
Dash Tabasco sauce
Dash Worcestershire sauce
1 tsp lemon juice
3 tbsp vodka
4 sticks celery to serve

1 Feed the tomatoes and onions through a juicer.

2 Stir in the Tabasco and Worcestershire sauces and lemon juice.

3 Stir in the vodka and serve over ice with a pair of celery sticks in each glass.

Note: Sprinkle a few mixed seeds over the drink for extra nutritional benefits.

Juicy Fruits

125ml/4floz/½ cup freshly squeezed
    orange juice
125ml/4floz/½ cup freshly pulped
    pineapple juice
4 tbsp tequila
75ml/3floz/⅓ cup lemon-flavored yogurt

1 Place all the ingredients in a blender and blend until smooth.

2 Pour into two tall glasses and serve.

Packed with antioxidants

Klamath blue green algae

Klamath blue green algae is full of nutrients that help to renourish the body if you have a drink or two too many. This drink is also packed with vitamin C, which helps the body to process alcohol faster. This is helpful for women, as the female body processes alcohol more slowly than the male body.

Wake Up

4 blood oranges
1 tsp Klamath blue green algae
12 medium strawberries, washed
   and hulled

1 Squeeze the juice from the oranges and place the juice and remaining ingredients in a blender.

2 Blend until smooth.

3 Pour over ice in glasses and serve.

Grapefruit Wake Up: Use 3 ruby grapefruit instead of the blood oranges.

Margarita

3 limes
Salt
4 tbsp tequila
2 tbsp triple sec or cointreau

1 Squeeze the juice from the limes with a citrus juicer or peel and feed through a juicer.

2 Dip the rim of two cocktail glasses into the lime juice, shaking the excess away, then dip them into salt.

3 Place the juice, tequila, and triple sec or cointreau in a blender or cocktail shaker and blend until well combined.

4 Pour into glasses and serve.

Frozen Margarita: Mix as above, then pour into a shallow container and freeze. To serve, scoop into a blender and whiz briefly.

Whisky and Raspberry Oat Smoothie

225g/8oz/1¾ cups fresh raspberries
125ml/4floz/½ cup orange juice
4 tbsp rolled oats
6–8 tbsp whisky

1 Reserve a few raspberries, then place all the ingredients in a blender and blend until smooth.

2 Serve poured over ice, and decorate with the reserved raspberries.

Whisky and Strawberry Oat Smoothie: Use strawberries in place of the raspberries.

Oats are a good source of **soluble fibre**, which can help lower cholesterol levels. Oats also help the body to use insulin, an important benefit for diabetics.

Gin, Elderflower, and Apple Fizz

Ice
125ml/4floz/½ cup gin
3 tbsp elderflower cordial or freshly
   squeezed orange juice
125ml/4floz/½ cup apple juice
1 tbsp lemon juice
225ml/8floz/1 cup sparkling water

1 Place a handful of ice in a blender
and add the gin, elderflower cordial,
apple juice, and lemon juice.

2 Blend to break up the ice.

3 Pour into glasses and top with
sparkling water.

**Brandy, Elderflower, and Apple
Fizz:** Use brandy instead of the gin.

Coffee and Almond Cream

125ml/4floz/½ cup strong black coffee
5 tbsp condensed milk
2–3 tbsp amaretto liqueur
2 tbsp double (heavy) cream

1 Place all the ingredients in a blender and blend until smooth.

2 Serve in chilled martini glasses for after-dinner luxury.

Creamy Whisky: Use whisky in place of the ameretto.

Cherry and Pomegranate Sparkle

125ml/4floz/½ cup cherry juice
125ml/4floz/½ cup pomegranate juice
Sparkling wine

1 Combine the cherry and pomegranate juices and pour into two glasses.

2 Top up with sparkling wine to taste.

Grape and Pomegranate Sparkle: Use red grape juice in place of the cherry juice.

jump up and touch the sky

Baileys Banana Crème

muscle energizer

4 tbsp Baileys cream liqueur
4 tbsp cold strong black coffee
4 tbsp single (light) cream
1 ripe banana, peeled

1 Place all the ingredients in a blender and blend until smooth.

2 Pour over ice and serve.

Iced Baileys Banana Crème: Replace the cream with 2 scoops of vanilla or coffee ice cream.

Bananas are one of the best sources for **potassium**, which helps your muscles to function properly. Bananas are also easy to digest, so a banana on its own is often recommended after an upset stomach.

Creamy Melon Whiz

4 tbsp banana liqueur
½ peeled banana
½ galia or cantaloupe melon, peeled, seeded, and cut into chunks
2 tbsp fromage frais (yogurt) or single (light) cream

1 Place all the ingredients in a blender and blend until smooth.

2 Serve poured over ice.

Brandy Melon Whiz: Use brandy instead of vodka.

More Melon

150g/5oz/1 cup watermelon, peeled,
   cut into chunks, and seeds discarded
¼ galia melon, peeled, seeded, and cut
   into chunks
6–8 tbsp vodka
Clear honey to taste (optional)

1 Reserve a few chunks of watermelon.
Place the melons in a blender and add
the vodka and honey if using.

2 Blend until smooth.

3 Pour into glasses and decorate with
the reserved fruit.

More Melon and Gin: Use gin instead
of vodka.

More Melon and Rum: Add white rum
instead of vodka.

Plum Brandy Nectar

8 plums, stoned
2 nectarines, stoned
4–6 tbsp brandy

1 Reserve a few slices of plum. Feed the nectarines and plums through a juicer.

2 Stir in the brandy.

3 Pour into glasses, decorate with the reserved plum slices, and serve.

Peach Brandy Nectar: Use peaches in place of the nectarines.

Apricot Brandy Nectar: Replace the nectarines with peaches and the plums with apricots.

Index

Acknowledgements

Thanks to Kenwood Ltd –
www.kenwoodworld.com – for
supplying their Smoothie Pro and
the Vita Proactive Juicer. Both
machines worked a treat for
testing the recipes in this book.

Also thanks to Nancy at the
Really Healthy Company –
www.healthy.co.uk – for advice
on nutritional supplements.

And to my friends in the SE1 book
club, who helped get this book
off to a flying start with a brain-
storming session of flavor
combination and juicing ideas.